George J. Adler

The Poetry of the Arabs of Spain

Being the Substance of a Lecture Read in the Small Chapel of the...

George J. Adler

The Poetry of the Arabs of Spain
Being the Substance of a Lecture Read in the Small Chapel of the...

ISBN/EAN: 9783744792394

Printed in Europe, USA, Canada, Australia, Japan

Cover: Foto ©Thomas Meinert / pixelio.de

More available books at **www.hansebooks.com**

OF

THE ARABS OF SPAIN.

Being the substance of a Lecture read in the small Chapel of the University

of the City of New York, on the evening of March 28th, 1867,

BY

G. J. ADLER, A. M.,

Late Professor of German to the University; Member of several Learned Societies.

———•••———

NEW YORK:

PRESS OF WYNKOOP & HALLENBECK,

No. 113 FULTON STREET, N. Y.

1867.

TO THE READER.

THE civilization of the Moslems of Spain has for the last quarter of a century been one of the most attractive themes of learned inquiry, and Science, History, Literature and Art have each been eager after new results, some of which Romance among us has sought to invest with the nimbus of its charms. Of late years their political history and that of their polite literature have more especially been favored with valuable contributions, partly in the shape of translations, partly in original works, from the pens of *savans* like Gayangos, de Slane, Dozy, Hammer-Purgstall, von Schack and others, and we have now an abundance of new light on matters heretofore known to but few or in the dim outlines of vague uncertainty. Leaving entirely aside the question of political history, except so far as it is interwoven with that of letters, I have endeavored, in the following pages, to give a brief survey of the immense field of the poetry of the Arabs of Spain,—a theme long familiar to us as one of fascinating romance, but known to us rather in generalities than in living specimens sufficient to give us a more or less adequate conception of its real character. From this sketch I could not very well exclude a summary recapitulation of the antecedents of this poetry, from its first crude tentatives of the desert to the date of the establishment of the Caliphate of the West; and these antecedents are fraught with so much interest, that it is hoped the reader will excuse it, if the porch should strike

him as not in strict harmony with the proportions of the
edifice. For the benefit of further inquiry, I subjoin
here also a list of the authorities upon which the little
work is based, and in which the student of Literary
History will find nearly all of any account that thus far
has been introduced to us.

1. Literaturgeschichte der Araber von ihrem Beginne bis zu Ende
des zwölften Jahrhunderts der Hidschret, von Hammer-Purgstall. 7 vols. 8vo. Wien, 1850–1856.

2. Poesie und Kunst der Araber in Spanien und Sicilien, von A.
F. von Schack. 2 vols. 12mo. Berlin, 1865.

3. Recherches sur l'Histoire et la Littérature de l'Espagne pendant
le Moyen Age, par R. Dozy. 2 vols. 8vo. Leyde, 1860.

4. Histoire des Musulmans d'Espagne jusqu'à la conquête de la
Andalousie par les Almoravides, par R. Dozy. 4 vols. 8vo.
Leyde, 1861.

5. Analectes sur l'Histoire et la Littérature des Arabes d'Espagne,
publiés par MM. Dozy, Dugal, Krehl et Wright. Leyde, 1861.

6. History of the Mohammedan Dynasties of Spain. From the
text of Ahmed Muhammed al Makkari. Translated by Pascual
de Gayangos. 2 vols. 4to. London, 1840.

7. Ibn Challikan's Biographical Dictionary, translated from the
Arabic by Baron Mac Guckin de Slane. 3 vols. 4to. Paris,
1843–45.

8. Prolégomènes Historiques d'Ibn Chaldun, traduits de l'arabe
par M. G. de Slane. 2 vols. 4to. Paris, 1862–65.

9. Histoire des Berbères et des Dynasties Musulmans d'Ibn Chai-
dun (arabe), par M. le baron de Slane. 2 vols. Algiers, 1847.

10. Journal Asiatique. Paris. 1830–1865.

I have in conclusion to express my acknowledgments
to a number of friends, at whose request and under whose
auspices my manuscript appears in type.

New York, August, 1867.

G. J. ADLER.

THE POETRY OF THE ARABS OF SPAIN.

The earliest poetical tentatives of the Arabs were improvisations, short epigrammatic pieces produced by the inspiration of the moment, and this appears to have been the only way in which the poetic talent of the nation displayed itself till toward the commencement of the sixth century of our era, near which time the art of writing was also introduced among them.

About that epoch, however, their genius in this direction developed itself with astonishing rapidity, and with such surprising success, that all the most celebrated masterpieces of the pre-islamitic period, and those that passed for classical at all times, were produced during the interval between the year 500 A. D. and the hegira (A. D. 622), *i. e.* within the space of less than a century and a quarter. It is true, that the different tribes quarrelled with one another about the priority of their distinguished names, but we have the decision of one of their own authorities to the effect that they all of them belonged to about the same epoch, and that the oldest of them could not have preceded the flight of the Prophet much more than a century.

The extent to which during this century poetry and the poets were held in esteem by the inhabitants of the Peninsula we may infer from the fact that the different tribes linked public exhibitions and recitations to the annual gatherings of their fairs—a ceremony for which the little palm-shaded town of Okadz, about three days' journey from Mecca, became more especially distinguished. The fair here was on the most sumptuous and extensive scale, and attended by crowds from every section of the country. It was held about the beginning of the three sacred months during which by an ancient custom every sort of warfare, bloodshed and revenge were religiously prohibited, and where the visitors were required to silence every hate. It was here that, in solemn public contest, the poets, who were most commonly also warriors, recited their verses, in which they generally undertook to celebrate either their own achievements, the renown of their ancestors, or the glory of their respective tribes. The poem, which won the prize on this occasion, was recorded on byssus in letters of gold, and then suspended from the walls of the Kaaba, the most ancient sanctuary of the sons of Ishmael, at Mecca. So runs at least an old tradition, which, although recently contested, has nevertheless considerable evidence in its favor. The seven great poems which constitute the body of the *Muallakat* (*i. e.* "the suspended"), were thus honored with the prize, and are at this day yet inviting our examination. In contradistinction to all the previous more primitive attempts of the sort, these poems no longer consist of but a few brief verses; they are compositions of more considerable dimensions, constructed with more artistic rhythm and rounded off into a more or less consistent whole. It is true, they are not pervaded by one dominant idea; they consist mostly of a series of emotions and descriptions rather loosely strung together; but amid all this disregard for strict unity of design, they yet exhibit at least a tendency to a definite aim, and in point of technical execution every part of them is constructed upon the same metre and with the same rhyme, the latter here extending itself to the middle as well as to the end of the verse (*beit*), which the Arabs invariably divided into two equal parts or hemistichs (*misra*). All these seven poems of the Muallakat belong to what the Arabs call the *kassîda*—a name applied to every regular poetic composition of from twenty to one hundred lines. In other respects this may then be either of the narrative or descriptive, the panegyric or satirical, the elegiac, the martial, or the amatory kind.

Now Okadz did not long remain the only place at which *fêtes* of the sort were instituted. As the love of poesy struck deeper root among the people, the *mufacharas* or public poetic recitations also became more general, and there was many an occasion on which the different tribes vied with each other in their attempts to produce the best poet, and to celebrate the victor with joyous demonstrations of every sort. The tribe even was congratulated for having produced a herald of its exploits to perpetuate its name among posterity. In a word, poetry now became one of the most vital elements of national existence, and that not only in the tents of the various chiefs or at the courts of the petty kings, but among all the members of the shiftless nomadic groups, which, as they roamed over the dreary waste of their unmeasured deserts, made the welkin ring with songs commemorating heroic courage, fidelity and love. The poet enjoyed a sort of patriarchal respect, wherever he went. He was not unfrequently constituted umpire for the adjustment of differences, and every one strove to win his favor or to avoid his displeasure.

Much of the poetry of this early pagan period presents a curious and striking contrast, or rather incongruity, of substance and of form. For, while on the one hand we encounter the most unlicensed passions of a barbaric age, and an almost unmitigated thirst for murder and revenge, we on the other, find all this invested with a subtilty of speech and a refined elegance of expression, as if the poem had been composed for no other object than that of illustrating a chapter of grammar or of rhetoric! Surprising as it may seem, the Arabs of the desert were most indefatigable and even critical students of their language, of which they not only made themselves grammatically masters, but were no less fastidious about the choice of words, the faultlessness of their rhymes and other points esteemed essential to excellence and purity of style. This was a study, to which they applied themselves from early youth, and which the poets kept up with unceasing vigilance as long as they composed. Let the following serve as an instance of perhaps extreme nicety on this point:—It once happened that two poets, Amrulkais and Alkama, engaged in a discussion with each other about their art, and entertained each other with the rehearsal of some of their own pieces. There being no umpire present, they agreed to make one of the wife of Amrulkais, and she was to decide which of the two deserved the precedence. The contest had no sooner commenced, than each one did his utmost to excel his rival, until the moment at last arrived to award the prize. The fair judge declared herself in favor of Alkama, on the ground that he had furnished the most successful description of the horse. The decision wounded her husband's poetic honor so much, that he at once insisted on divorce, and the affair ended by her getting married to his rival. (Caussin de Perceval, vol. i., p. 314, 345.)

The pre-islamitic poetry of the Arabs, as far as it has come cown to us, is preserved mainly in the four collections of the Muallakat, the Hamasa, the Divan of the Hudseilites (a tribe long at war with the Koreishites), and the Great Book of Songs (*Kitab el aghani*). Let us now briefly survey the leading points to be considered first in regard to the Muallakat and then concerning the remaining collections of this period.

In glancing at the different kassîdas of the Muallakat, we are at once struck with the observation, that none of them transcend the limits of a certain circle of ideas, and that this circle is itself a somewhat circumscribed one. The cause of this is obvious enough. The Arab had neither a mythology nor epic traditions, like the Oriental or the Greek, and in his attempt to make poetry was restricted either to the expression of his personal emotions or to the delineation of the circumstances of life and nature by which he was surrounded. And here even he limited himself to mere descriptions; for he remained a stranger to the drama, as well as to the epos, and that not only at this early period, but at every epoch of his history. We need not therefore be surprised to meet with the almost incessant recurrence of the same objects in nearly every one of these compositions, as for example, the perils of a march through the desert, a collision with some hostile tribe, the description of a horse. camel or gazelle, of a thunderstorm or hurricane, the celebration of the charms of the poet's lady-love or of the excellence of his arms, and the like. Of all this we encounter more or less in every one of the kassidas of the Muallakat, and yet we cannot accuse them either of monotony or of a want of interest. The keen observation of the Arab considers these few objects from a thousand different points of view, and his prolific invention invests them with a bold novelty, a variety and freshness, which never fail to touch the imagination and the heart.

The names linked to the seven kassidas of the Muallakat are Shanfara, Antar, Tarafa, Ibn Kultum, Tuhair, Amrulkais, and Lebid. Of the lives of these poets we know but very little, and it is not of much moment that we should. Let it suffice for our purpose to give in outline a specimen or two of their poetry. The kassida of Shanfara delineates with masterly touches the hero of the desert in all his native, although savage, grandeur. At variance with all the world, he at the hour of midnight moves out into the desert, where he then hails the fierce panther and the shaggy hyæna as his friends. Stretched out upon the hard and sun-seared ground, with no other companion but his trusty bow, his flashing sword and his own dauntless heart, he takes his sole delight in solitude, which offers the hero refuge against the envy and jealousy of his rivals. In many a cold night he has fearlessly advanced through the howling storm and darkness, attended by hunger and by every thing calculated to inspire terror. He has made many a woman a widow and many a child an orphan. But he has met with nothing but ingratitude from the brethren of his tribe; it is this which has produced his present aversion to men, and he now bids welcome to the monsters of the desert, which never betray a friend or carelessly blab out his secrets. He is resolved henceforth to live among the slender-bodied wolves which plunge through the ravines with the rapidity of the wind. He chooses them, because they are brave and defiant like himself!—The kassída of Lebid, the last of these ancient poets, is a no less curious little *genre*-sketch of the life of the old Arabs. He boasts of himself as always on the alert for the defense of his tribe from his watch-post on the hill-top, whence he may observe every movement of the enemy, and whence their standards even are enveloped by the clouds of dust arising from his horse's hoofs. At his tent the traveller always finds shelter against the chills of the morning, when the reins of the winds are in the hands of the icy North. No poor woman, impelled by hunger to seek his protection, has ever been refused the comforts of his frugal home. The poet then gives us an earnest lesson on the inconstancy of all things here below, and on the evanescence of our own brief span of life. We pass away, while the stars rising on the sky remain permanent, and the mountains and palaces surpass us in duration. No mortal can escape from the allotments of his Fate, and when his hour strikes, he falls. It is with men as it is with camps and those that occupy them ; if the latter move away the former remain desolate. Man is but a flash of lightning or a flame, and is reduced to ashes the moment the light expires.—Lebid was the last of the seven authors of the Muallakat, and lived long enough to have an interview with the Prophet, which is curious enough to deserve at least a passing notice. Mohammed's preaching had already produced a great sensation, and while many were yet doubting and even deriding his pretensions, there were many others who were no less anxious to ascertain the truth. Among the latter were the members of Lebid's tribe, and they knew no better way to satisfy themselves than that of commissioning the old poet to inquire in their behalf. The latter went and found the Prophet in the act of haranguing an assembly in a most eloquent discourse, in which he happened to repeat a portion of the second *sura*. The passage, which is an extremely forcible one, produced so powerful an effect on our poet, that he declared his *muallaka* surpassed, and resolved to renounce his art for ever, to embrace Islam in its stead.

We must not allow this incident, however, to mislead us in respect to the influence of the Koran on the subsequent development of Arabic poetry ; for this influence was rather a general than a special one, and on that account remained much more limited than we might be inclined to suspect. Lebid's poetical successors were doubtless all of them Moslems without reproach, schooled in their sacred book from early youth and ready to defend their faith on every occasion, even with the sword, but we nevertheless find them at all times looking up to their predecessors of the olden time as the great masters of their art, whom they considered it possible only to rival but never to surpass, as in respect to the language also they considered the desert with its old poets the only school from which to learn, and on that account often left distant courts and provinces to study among the Beduins of the cradle of their faith.

The remaining collections of the pagan period, that is to say, the Hamasa, the Divan of the Hudseilites and others, offer us a much larger number of pieces, mostly, however, of smaller dimensions, but of much more varied contents than the kassidas. We have here strung together side by side poetical effusions of every class, heroic songs, lays of the martial and the amatory kind (*ghasels*), dirges and satires, sportive and convivial songs. Many of these pieces evince no small degree of lyrical elevation ; they offer us a multitude of striking similes, a surprising versatility of construction and a certain bold abruptness of style. Nevertheless, the Arab here likewise neither did nor could transcend the horizon of his circumscribed ideas, and the subjects and sentiments of all these compositions never pass beyond the limited circle of his particular mode of life. Demonstrations of indignation at the wounded honor of his tribe, invectives against an enemy, expressions of sorrow and menaces of revenge over the murder of a relative or friend, exultation over feats of prowess amid some perilous encounter, exhortations to courage, with now and then an apophthegm or sage maxim of life, and occasionally also sentiments of a humaner sort, such as regretful sighs addressed to a distant love whose image does not cease to visit him in his dreams,—such are most commonly the themes which inspire the poet of this period, and on which he expends all the ingenuity and art of which his genius was capable.

The introduction of Islam produced a complete revolution in the intellectual condition of the Arab and gave his entire life and character not only a new direction, but an elevation and expansion for which we can scarcely find a parallel in history. While in his primitive condition his ideas were determined wholly by the impulse of the moment and the circumstances by which he found himself surrounded, the unrivalled eloquence of the Prophet suddenly broke down the limits of time and space by pointing the dazzled hearer on the one hand to the seven heavens above with the felicity of the Blessed, and on the other to the unfathomed pool below, ready to engulf the unbeliever in its flames. He was introduced to Allah, the only One and the Supreme, the terror of the perverse and the munificent rewarder of the observers of his law. The delights of the Paradise, more especially held out to the believer, were of the most enchanting and transcendent kind, and operated with the influence of magic on the naturally material motives of the Arab's mind. The Koran was therefore no sooner fairly introduced among the different tribes than it at once became the foundation of their entire culture, and so powerful was the inspiration of its doctrines, that they were ready not only to defend them as a divine revelation but even to enforce their recognition with the point of the lance in every portion of the world. Islam thus became synonymous with conquest, and the stern Beduin of the desert in an almost incredibly short time made himself the military suzerain of immense territories, the builder of castles, palaces and cities without number, the founder of dynasties, and the possessor of all the luxuries and refined material enjoyments that can convert life into an almost literal realization of his dreams of Paradise. It was thus that within a century of the hegira (A. D. 622–722) the empire of the caliphs won an expansion, such as none, either before or after, ever could boast of in history, extending at times towards the East as far as the confines of China, and in the West not only over the whole of the north of Africa and over Spain, but sometimes even beyond the Pyrenees as far as the Garonne. The first seat of the new government was Medina, where Mohammed died in A. D. 633, and where his successor ruled until 660. In that year Damascus became the capital of the caliphate with the accession of the Ommaiades, who made that city their residence until the fall of the dynasty in A. D. 718. In 775 Bagdad was preferred by the Abbassides, who retained that as the seat of their dynasty until the extinction of the chaliphate of the East in A. D. 1258. In the West the petty *melcks* or kings for more than a century remained tributary to the Prophet's successor at Damascus, until their own dissensions and the many alternations of the war led to the establishment of the rival caliphate of the West in A. D. 749. The founder of this dynasty was Abdurrahman, a scion of the Ommaiades, who upon the accession of the Abbassides in the East, had alone been fortunate enough to escape from the atrocious massacre of his kinsmen and to find his way into Spain. The centre of the Western Caliphate, which was one of great power and splendor, was Cordova (750–1027). After its dissolution, the Moslem provinces of Spain were again ruled by a number of petty kings, among whom we must more especially mention those who resided at Granada and Seville. The dominion of the Arabs in Spain, counting from the first invasion, lasted from A. D. 711 until 1492, that is to say, within a few years of eight centuries. The last stern defender of Islam upon the soil of Spain was Abul Hassan of Granada, and his son Boabdil the last Moorish king, expelled by Ferdinand the Catholic in 1492.

One might suppose that so complete a change of sentiment and life as that introduced by the new religion, and the perpetual din of arms with the intoxication of success attending the first conquests, would have entirely hushed the voice of the old poetry of the Arabs, at least for a considerable time. But this was far from being the case. For, in the first place, we find not only poets, but poets of the court even, directly after the establishment of the caliphate of Damascus, and in the second place, the Koran, although worshiped as the great text-book at once of the religion and of the education of the Moslem, and venerated as a model of eloquence not to be surpassed or even approached, nevertheless can not be said to have either radically changed or even seriously modified the poetics of the Arabs, who in this respect continued to cling to their antecedents of the Muallakat and of the Divan. The extent to which this was the case is best illustrated by the following little incident:—The celebrated Feresdak, chancing one day to overhear a passer-by repeating a passage from Lebid's muallaka, prostrated himself upon the ground, as if in prayer, and when interrogated about the cause of this, he replied, " Ye others recite passages from the Koran, at which ye expect us to fall down ; I am acquainted with verses to which the same homage is due." And this was not the sentiment of an individual only, or of a particular epoch ; it was the general one at all times, and there were even those who went to the extreme of pronouncing all the poetry of the islamitic period but a feeble echo of that of the earlier golden age.

The dynasty of the Ommaiades no sooner was fairly established on its throne, than it already retained regularly paid poets permanently at its court. One of the main duties of these poets was avowedly that of the celebration of the sovereign at whose residence they were thus honored, and their kassidas are therefore mostly of the panegyric kind. The poet generally begins with allusions to his lady-love and to her former place of residence; he next describes the journey which is to conduct him to the presence of his Mæcenas, and then concludes with a most elaborately pompous eulogy of the suzerain. The importance attached to pieces of this sort by the rulers of the East was often very great, and there are instances in which a single happy expression or a memorable verse relating to their praise became an object of no little jealousy among them.

The number of poets, which flourished during the first century of the new era, was already very considerable, and the respect and influence which the most prominent of them enjoyed among the nation at large, was often an immense one. Indeed, it not unfrequently happened that their favor was courted, as if it were a royal one, and the displeasure of their verses dreaded as that of the most deadly enemy. All classes of society were pervaded by a veritable passion for the noble art, which neither the clash of arms nor the wild fanaticism, which at that time was in full blaze to disseminate the new law over the entire world, were able to silence or suppress. We thus find, that even amid the noisiest alarms of war the comparative merit of two rival poets was discussed with a zeal that scarcely could be surpassed, had the question turned upon the most important affair of state, and that on the eve of a battle and in the presence of two armies a public duel was to be fought to decide the question, as to whether Djerir or Feresdak was the greater poet of the two. This Djerir and Feresdak together with Achtal enjoyed the fame of being the most distinguished representatives of their art during the first century; and of this they themselves appear to have been so well aware, that each of them looked upon himself as the superior not only of his rivals but even of his predecessors,—an evidence that an excess of modesty was not among their foibles or their virtues, as it in fact rarely was among any of the poets of the Moslem faith. For the rest, however, Djerir seems to have been the most successful of the three, and he could boast of himself as unsurpassed in every department of poetry, while the rest excelled only in a special branch. A kassida, composed in honor of the caliph, pleased, we are told, the latter so well, that he promised the poet five hundred camels for his reward. Djerir, however, not satisfied yet, expressed his apprehension, that they might run away, unless they had a keeper. "Very well, then," replied the caliph, "I'll give you eight slaves to watch them." "Then, Emir of the Faithful, I need nothing more than a vessel into which to milk them," added the poet, keeping his eye riveted upon a golden bowl, which he found standing in the hall, and the magnanimity of his illustrious patron could not well refuse to add this costly present to the rest. (Journal Asiatique, 1834, No. ii., p. 18, 22).

As a part of the material organization of Moslem poetry we must not forget to mention a particular class of men, analogous to the *jongleurs* of the Provençals, by the Arabs called *rawias,* whose business consisted in reciting and disseminating the works of their poets among the nation at large. They were accustomed to move as itinerants from place to place, and their rehearsals were devoured by crowds of eager listeners everywhere. Some of them are reported to have been such prodigies of memory, that the stories told of them border on the incredible. It will be enough for our purpose to make room for one. Caliph Al Walid once happening to ask *rawia* Hammad how many poems he knew by heart, the latter replied: " I can repeat to you for every letter of the alphabet one hundred long kassídas, all of them rhyming with the letter, to say nothing of the many shorter pieces. And all these kassídas are of the pagan age, to which I might add many an other from the days of Islam." Challenged to verify his boast, he then recited to the caliph's representative (for the prince himself might have grown weary of the trial) no less than two thousand nine hundred kássídas from the pagan time, and was rewarded with the munificent present of one hundred thousand dirhems for the feat.

But not content with the mere recital of their poetry, the Arabs also sung much of it, especially the minor pieces, probably of the amatory kind, to the sound of various instruments. The art of music had anciently been much in vogue among them, and although some of the more fastidious believers for a time made objections to it from the writings of the Prophet, it yet soon not only recovered but even surpassed its former popularity, and the palaces of the caliphs were resonant with the merry notes of the human voice, and of the lute and cithern. The number of singers of both sexes during the first century and a half was very great, and we have even biographies left of many of them. Most of them were either of Persian origin or had been educated in their art by Persian masters, to whom the Moslems thus probably became indebted for nearly all the new improvements in this respect. The most celebrated of these singers were Mabed and Assa ul Meila, the latter of whom enjoyed the reputation of being the princess of all the players on the cithern and the lute, while Mabed was allowed to boast against a general of having composed the music to seven songs, for each of which he claimed an honor superior to that of the capture of a fortress; and so little opposition did his pretension meet with, that the seven melodies subsequently acquired the appellation of Mabed's fortresses.

Such then was, briefly, the state of poetry and music under the Eastern Caliphate until about the extinction of the Ommaiades in A. D. 817. The accession of the next dynasty, that of the Abbassides, initiated but a new career of splendor, superior even to the first; but this we are here not at liberty to trace, it being now high time for us to turn our attention to the West, to the new Caliphate of the Ommaiades at Cordova, which from about this date for upward of two centuries divided the power and the glory of the Moslem world. Before the arrival of Abdurrahman, the Arabs of Spain were too much diverted by the war to have much leisure or inclination for poetry or any of the fine arts, but under the auspices of this prince and his illustrious successors the whole of the civilization of the East was successfully transplanted upon western soil, where it soon began to rival whatever there was of refinement and intelligence, of luxury and splendor at the Eastern court, and where it continued to flourish with a few transient interruptions until the extinction of the Moorish domination in Spain. Before proceeding now to survey the poetry of the West, it will not be out of place to give a brief outline of the general state of letters and the arts, as cultivated and introduced by the princes of this noble line.

Abdurrahman and his immediate successors contributed to the material advancement of the nation on the most extensive and magnificent scale. During their reign, Cordova grew up into the largest city of the West, with its one hundred and thirteen thousand houses (exclusive of the palaces and other public buildings), its twenty-eight suburbs and its three thousand mosques. In every direction from the city, the valley of the Guadalquivir was checkered with palaces and villas, with extensive gardens and charming places of public resort, inviting the inhabitants to their refreshing shade. A huge bridge was thrown across the river, and the immense mosque constructed whose grandeur and magnificence were for centuries the object of admiration and of pious visit to believers from every portion of the world. The court of Abdurrahman II. vied in luxurious splendor with that of Bagdad, and at his behest numberless palaces, mosques, aqueducts, bridges, and other public works arose in rapid succession over every part of Andalusia. Under Abdurrahman III., who was the first to assume the title of Caliph

2

of the West, the Kingdom of Andalusia reached its zenith of
material prosperity, and the genius of this magnanimous prince
made that prosperity the basis of so high an intellectual culture,
that the writers of the West and East never grew weary of
speaking in terms of rapture of his character and influence.

The general education of the nation, as well as the advancement of the sciences and arts, was conducted with still greater
zeal and with the most brilliant success by the next following
caliph, Hakem II., under whose auspices the public institutions
of his kingdom attained to a degree of perfection, such as they
had never seen before, and such as probably at that time scarce
existed anywhere else either in the West or East. While in the
rest of Europe scarcely any one, except the clergy, knew how
to read and write, Andalusia, and in fact the whole of Moorish
Spain, had schools without number, in which the art was generally taught, and Hakem gave his capital alone twenty-seven
for the special purpose of educating the children of the poorer
classes free of expense. Nor was there any lack of institutions
of a higher grade; there were numerous academies, generally
attached to the mosques, at Cordova, Seville, Toledo, Valencia,
Almeria, Malaga and Jaen, at which the superior disciplines
were taught, such as the interpretation of the Koran, philology,
the mathematics, astronomy, medicine, jurisprudence and philosophy, and the halls of which attracted both hearers and pro-
fessors from all parts of the Mohammedan, and after a while
also from the Christian, world. So general was the taste and
even the zeal for studies, that as these Spanish institutions were
frequented by students from the remotest parts of Asia and the
heart of Germany, the Andalusians on their part would frequently not shun the hardships of the long journey to the East
to quench their thirst for knowledge in the lecture-room of
some distinguished master at Tunis, Cairwan, Cairo, Damascus,
Bagdad, Mecca, Bassora or Cufa, and there are instances on
record in which such learned pilgrimages extended as far as
India and China, and into the very heart of Africa.

But not content with the mere *viva vox* of knowledge, Hakem
was determined to possess it in a more permanent form; he
founded a library for which his agents were commissioned to
make collections in every part of the world, until the number
of its volumes, for which he made room in his palace at Cordova, had risen to the enormous figure of four hundred thousand.
And all the books of this immense collection, it is asserted, were
read or consulted by the Caliph himself, and many of them
enriched with marginal notes from his own hand. The *personnel*

of this library included a number of the most skillful copyists
and binders, who occupied themselves constantly with the
multiplication or the restoration of the precious manuscripts.
Hakem's court thus soon became the natural resort for all the
genius of the nation, and his liberality towards men of letters is
said to have known no bounds. The intellectual life developed
under the benign auspices of this prince was therefore naturally
and in every respect a most brilliant one, and there is no example
like it anywhere in the Middle Age. Nor was the *hadjib* or
chamberlain of Hakem's impotent successor, the great Almansor,
indifferent to science, but encouraged and rewarded merit in
every one, except that his religious fanaticism restricted the
liberty of speech in matters of philosophy, to which before him
there had been no restraint.

The capture of Cordova by the Berbers in 1013 scattered
Hakem's immense collection of books, all of which were then
either destroyed or sold. The downfall of the Caliphate, however, so far from burying beneath its ruins the civilization it
had so successfully initiated and advanced, gave rise to a new
period of literary history, in every respect equal, if not superior, to that which had preceded. The numerous independent
states, which formed themselves out of the dismembered empire,
became as many centres of intellectual light, of learned and
artistic culture. The small dynasties of Seville, Granada,
Toledo, Badajoz and Almeria vied with each other in their zeal
for the advancement of the sciences and arts, and drew within
their circles crowds of authors, artists and other men of
genius or talent, which then either received regular salary
or costly presents for the dedication of their works.* At
all of these courts, the intellect, even in matters of spec-
ulative philosophy, enjoyed a degree of freedom, such as
in some parts of Europe the nineteenth century does not yet

* In connection with this patronage there was undoubtedly often much
servility. We have, however, already met with instances of no small
degree of independence, and the following is one which may well pass for a
literary curiosity. An eminent philologian by the name of Abu Galib happened to attract the attention of Mudjahid the king of Denia, who promised him a horse, a superb suit of armor, and one thousand pieces of gold,
if he would honor him with the dedication of one of his works. But the
author promptly declined the present together with the honor by saying:
"I have written my book, to be of service to mankind and to make my
name immortal; and why should I now adorn it with the name of another
and thus transfer the fame of it to him? No! I shall never do it!" The
emir, who was a sensible man, no sooner heard of the reply, than, so far
from being offended, he expressed admiration for the *savant's* independence,
and sent him double the amount of the promised gift.

seem prepared to boast of. Some of the princes of these houses themselves participated, like the caliphs, in the general emulation, and even won celebrity either as poets, philosophers or authors of some other kind. Such were, for example, El Moktadir of Saragossa, El Mutsaffir of Badajoz, some of the Abbadides of Sevilla, of the Benu Somadih of Almeria and others. It is true, that this state of things was not unfrequently menaced partly by the advances of the Christian armies, and sometimes also by the fanaticism of the Moorish allies called in from Africa to aid against them, yet it may nevertheless be said to have lasted with no material interruption until the very end of the Moslem rule in Spain. Under the Almohades, especially under Abdulmunen and his successor Jussuf, Cordova once more regained some of its former glory, as a seat of letters and a place for books, and about this time its academies could boast of men no less eminent than Averroës, Abenzoar and Abu Bacer, who long before our own revival of letters drew the writings of Aristotle (although, it is maintained, only in Syriac translations) from their oblivion, and with their bold philosophical researches won themselves not only an immense cotemporary celebrity, but a permanent place in the history of philosophy. In regard to books, it has been ascertained that as late as the thirteenth century the different cities of Andalusia contained no less than seventy libraries open to the public (Journal Asiatique, 1838, No. IV., p. 73).

When in 1236 the grand mosque of Cordova was surmounted by the Christian cross and soon after Sevilla also surrendered to the king of Castile, the dominion of the Arabs found itself reduced to much narrower limits, and the kingdom of Granada now became the only seat of power left them. This little kingdom, however, continued to maintain in the most creditable manner the *prestige* of Moslem civilization intact for at least two centuries and a half after the fall of Cordova, and most of its princes, after the example of Mohammed Ben Ahmar, not only zealously kept up their schools and libraries, but generously opened their court as an asylum to the many unfortunate men of genius or learning expelled from conquered quarters. Granada thus still remained, and to the very last, the seat of no small degree of literary culture, which was yet possessed of vitality enough to survive even the fall of the Moorish dominion in Spain for some time after upon the soil of Africa.

The centre and the soul of all this astonishing development of intellectual life in Moorish Spain was, we may say it without exaggeration, poetry, which for at least six centuries was cultivated with so much zeal and by so large a number, that a mere register of all the Arabic poets of the Peninsula would fill entire folios. The taste for it had by the middle of the ninth century already become so general, that not only the Arabs, but even some of the Christians subject to their sway, occupied themselves with making verses in the idiom of Islam. About a century later we already begin to meet with anthologies, as for example, "The Gardens" of Ibn Ferradj, the two hundred chapters of which (each chapter of one hundred distichs) were exclusively devoted to pieces from the pens of Andalusian authors. This collection was soon followed by numerous others, of which some professed merely to complete it, while others made the necessary additions for the next following centuries. Such were more especially those of Ibn Bessam and of Ibn Chakan, which for a long time circulated widely as the most complete and popular. We need not be surprised therefore to find, that under influences like these poetry should have allied itself so intimately not only with the social relations, but even with the daily industrial occupations and enterprises of the nation, and that as the princes sometimes did not disdain to emulate each other, and even the poets in the art of making verses, so the very peasant of the field took pleasure in his ingenious improvisations, and the man behind the plough would sometimes boast of his ability to spin out his rhymes on any given theme. Among the caliphs and the princes the talent, or at any rate the attempt, was so general, that there is yet extant a work exclusively devoted to the kings and nobles of Andalusia, who excelled in this respect. Nor were the ladies deficient either in ambition or success, and the women of the harem not unfrequently contested the prize with men. Poetical inscriptions upon the walls and pillars of the palaces, which were often very ingeniously executed, constituted one of their most valued ornaments. The cavalier needed a verse or two for the blade of his scimitar, and there was no dull novelist or historian who could refrain from spicing his pages with some metrical citations or fragments of his own. The talent for poetry was not unfrequently the passport by which men from the lowest ranks rose to the highest offices of state, and to princely influence and fortune. Verses were employed to give emphasis or *éclat* to diplomatic transactions; sometimes they became the signal for bloody conflict, as also then again the charm to mitigate the victor's wrath. A single happy improvisation is known to have saved the life of more than one condemned, and to have burst the bolts of prisons. Rhyme-duels between two combatants in the presence of their respective armies were among the most common occurrences of warfare, while poetic challenges, as an exercise of wit, constituted one of the standing amusements of daily life. Of epistolary correspondence in verse between friends and lovers there is also no lack of evidence. In a word, the ability to express one's self in rhyme passed for one of the most coveted accomplishments, and the mania insinuated itself even into works of science and into papers of state.

As in the East, so also at Cordova, we meet with several poets who made themselves more especially conspicuous at court. Under the earlier caliphs, there was, in the first place, Yahyah, surnamed also from his personal appearance El Gazal (*i. e.* the gazelle), who was honored with several important embassies, and whose polished refinement of manners and conversation made him welcome everywhere. While at Constantinople, the emperor expressed the wish to retain him in his service, but he excused himself by saying that he could not keep him company, on account of his inability to drink wine with him. One day upon the appearance of the empress, he professed himself completely vanquished by her charms, which he then went on to celebrate in the most glowing terms,—a flattery which raised him still higher in the estimation of both their majesties. When on another mission to the king of the Normans, he produced an equally good impression by improvising some felicitous verses on the great beauty of Queen Theuda. At a later date, however, he was obliged to wander into exile on account of some satirical verses, which gave offense to Abdurrahman II., and then went to Bagdad, where his ingenuity and *ésprit* soon succeeded in overcoming completely the fastidious prejudice against the poetry of the West, still in vogue there. In connection with the court of Abdurrahman II., we have more especially to notice a singer by the name of Ziryab from Bagdad, who had come to Cordova on special invitation. His reception was of the most flattering description; a superb mansion was assigned to him, while his revenue in money and other allowances was equal to that of a prince; and princely also was the display he made of it, he never appearing in public without the attendance of one hundred slaves. But Ziryab was far from being a mere singer of the ordinary kind; he had travelled extensively, had studied poetry, astronomy, history, and art, was a man of taste and wit, and his conversations on every branch of knowl-

23

edge were so fascinating and instructive, that the caliph chose him for his most intimate associate. In his own art, he knew the words and tunes of ten thousand songs by heart; and his singing was so enchanting, that the report obtained of his receiving nightly visitations from *genii*, instructing him in melodies. The court of Abdurrahman III. boasted of the names of Ibn Abdrebbihi and Moudhir Ibn Saïd, from the latter of whom the caliph received a most important service at the reception of an embassy. It once happened that some envoys from Constantinople had arrived, and they were received in the magnificently decorated hall destined for that purpose. On their delivering their credentials and messages in solemn state, the caliph called upon the most prominent of his *sarans* present to reply in an address commemorating the glory of Islam and the honor of the caliphate; but they unfortunately all lost their presence of mind and wretchedly failed, when all at once our poet rose and delivered a long poetical harangue, by which the entire audience was transported with admiration, and for which the monarch then munificently rewarded him with a high office of state.[*] Nor were the auspices of Almansur any the less favorable to poetry and the poets, in connection with whom he kept up regular literary *conversazione* at his palace, and allowed them to accompany him even on his military expeditions. Such were, for example, Ibn Derradj, Yussuf ar Ramadi, and Saïd, of whom the latter more especially rose to high consideration by a variety of pleasing compliments, among others by some ingenious couplets composed upon the capture of Count Garcia Fernandez of Castile. Saïd, however, had some jealous rivals, who attempted to defame him with the charge of plagiarism. But he stood the trial imposed upon him by Almansur so much to his credit, as only to receive additional honors and rewards for it.

[*] In connection with the first caliph, we can scarcely avoid adding the following pleasant little anecdote:—Abdurrahman happening to be ill, it was declared necessary that he should be bled. He was seated in the great hall of the pavilion, which surmounted the heights of Az-Zähra, and the physician was just at the point of applying his instrument to the caliph's arm, when suddenly a starling came flying in, and after alighting upon a golden vase close by, gave utterance to the following verses:

" O thou, who with the lancet art now about to shed the blood of the Emir of the Faithful, be careful, mind now, be careful of the illustrious vein, in which the life of worlds is circulating !"

The starling repeated the couplet several times to the great amusement of the caliph, who expressed his astonishment and desired to know who taught the bird the verses. On learning that Murdshana, the mother of the crown-prince El Hakem, was the author of the ingenious device, he rewarded her with a magnificent present for the entertainment she had arranged for him. (El Makkari, ed. Gayangos, vol. i., p. 232).

The dismemberment of the caliphate gave rise to a new phase in the literary life of the Moorish bards, and one which bore much resemblance to that of the troubadours of Christian Europe. The poets now commenced to move from place to place, and there was probably no petty court, no castle or palace of prince or noble, which did not covet their association, and receive them as the honored guests of its refined society. This society had now become a much freer one than that which existed subject to the restraint of high court etiquette, and it was on that account extremely favorable to a generous interchange of thought and to a high degree of intellectual culture. The poets had many more Mæcenases to celebrate, and the latter were rarely wanting in the ambition to appreciate and reward them. The charming sky of Andalusia was of itself enough to dispose even the obtuser mind to the delightful intercourse of song and poesy, and the enchanting moonlight-evenings in some sequestered palace garden naturally invited to the recital of some fairy Oriental tale or to ingenious poetical improvisations, while the soft evening breezes wafted coolness from the fountains and fragrance from the flowers around the merry company, or the cup circulated freely among them, directed perhaps and socially partaken of by the high hand itself that gave the entertainment. The manners and customs of these small courts were thus in many respects identical with those of our own mediæval chivalry, and there are not wanting those who on that account are inclined to refer the origin of that institution to the Moslems and the East. Without being at all disposed or willing to defend this theory, we are yet ready to admit that many of the ideas and principles characteristic of chivalry, as for example that of honor and of gallantry, may be traced among the Arabs as far back as the time of their earliest antiquity. The respect for woman and her protection, the glory of perilous achievements, the defense of the weak or the oppressed, and the punctilious exaction of revenge, constituted the main characteristics of the otherwise lawless old Beduin of the desert, and this was the magic circle to which his entire life belonged. The chivalry of the Moslems, therefore, developed itself doubtless from its own resources, and we must also add as incontestable, that the spirit and refinement of it showed itself some centuries earlier among them than among the warriors of Christian Europe.

The poetry of Moorish Spain differs upon the whole but little, either in point of form or character, from that of the

East, except perhaps as far as it was modified imperceptibly by the influence of climate and of sky, and that not only because there was identity of origin, but also because the intellectual commerce between the colony and the mother country was, as we have seen, an uninterrupted and often a very lively one. Now this may be asserted as correct in spite of the circumstance that the same can not be affirmed of the language, which in the mouth of the Andalusian soon lost so much of its native purity as gradually to degenerate into an ungrammatical dialect, so that the Beduin of the desert (who by the way always remained the authority of it) might have found fault with the speech of a Moor in other respects much superior to him. The fact was, that the deterioration in question affected rather the speech than the written language of the Spanish Moslem, who in his youth was made familiar, not only with his Koran, but quite commonly also with his grammar and the poets, and if he made pretentions to superior education would have incurred the censure of good society, had he not been able to recite at least a certain number (and this was not unfrequently quite considerable) of elegant extracts from the classical writers of his nation in poetry and prose. If he professed to be a poet, or intended to become one, he would subject himself to a severer discipline and a more extensive course on literature, nor would he ever consider himself at liberty to neglect his Hamasa or his Muallakat. We need not therefore be surprised to find that the poets of the West generally showed no lack either of correctness or of elegance, and that the most prominent of their number never failed of being recognized by their rivals in the East, as in every respect their peers. Ibn Zeidun thus acquired the epithet of "the Bothori of the West," while Ibn Hani, Ar-Remmadi and Ibn Derradj were each of them honored as "the Montenebbi of the Occident," and Montenebbi himself, on hearing the poems of a Spaniard recited, is said to have exclaimed with enthusiastic admiration: "This people is really possessed of genius for poetry!"*

The subjects treated by the poets of the West no longer revolve within the narrow circle of the Beduins of the desert, but correspond in point of variety and multiplicity with the expanded relations of a more advanced civilization. The different

---

* Montenebbi wrote very early in life, and his conceit at one time misled him into aspiring after a new prophetship (whence his name the "Pretender to the Prophetship"). He found himself, however, three centuries too late, and was obliged to remain content a poet. And he nevertheless really was one in every sense.

collections therefore offer us multitudes of pieces of every description and dimension, and from numberless authors,—lays
of the chivalrous and amatory kind, poems relating to the sacred
wars, panegyrics and satires, pieces descriptive of nature or of
works of art, elegies and religious poems, drinking-songs, epigrams, besides a variety of popular forms and miscellaneous
specimens that can not well be classified. We now propose to
pass the most important of these rubrics briefly in review.

The position of woman in the society of Moslem Spain seems
to have been a freer one than elsewhere among the Mohammedans, and she was permitted to be a sharer of the whole intellectual culture of her time. Hence we find quite a number of
those who either won distinction in the sciences or vied with the
men in the art of making poetry. This superiority of education gave rise to a degree and kind of respect such as the East
scarcely knew, where the sentiment of love, for example, was
almost exclusively based on merely physical charms, and the
relation between the sexes thus became a much superior one.
Talent and knowledge were regarded as attractions in no
respect inferior to those of personal beauty, and it was not unfrequently the case that a common taste for music or poetry constituted an intimate bond of union between two hearts. We need
not therefore be surprised, when in the amatory poetry of the
Spanish Arabs we occasionally meet with an intensity of feeling,
a mixture of impetuous passion and of tender melancholy, such as
our Middle Age scarcely can produce an instance of, and which
is much closer allied to the sentimentality of modern times.
Nevertheless, however true all this may be, we will yet not
undertake to deny that much of the amatory poetry of the Moors
is pervaded by the voluptuous element to a much greater extent than good taste is now willing to admit, and we shall
on that account not dwell on it. We will content ourselves
with a few specimens of the purer sort.

The following love-epistle addressed to his lady-love by
Prince Izzuddaula is destitute neither of ingenuity nor of delicacy of sentiment:

" In mourning and with longing sighs have I composed for thee this letter, my love; and had my heart but courage, how fain would I myself become the bearer of my message."

" Imagine, in perusing now these lines, myself as coming from a distance,
and the black letters to be the pupils of my own dark eyes."

" Permit my kisses to be imprinted on the little note, the seal of which, O
dearest one on earth, is destined presently to be dissolved by thy white,
tender fingers." (Dozy's Recherches, p. 111.)

The following ghasel from the pen of Crown-prince Abdurrahman has reference to the idea of meeting in dreams, quite frequently treated by the Moorish poets :

"Let her be greeted, who never deigned to requite me with a solitary word ; who never to the warmest salutations of my heart sent me the least consoling answer."

" Let the gazelle be greeted, who thus reciprocates my inclination as cruelly to transfix me with her looks, which wound like lightly feathered arrows."

"Ah, she has never given me hope or balm to heal my aching sorrow, has never to my slumbers sent her lovely image to encourage." (Von Schack, vol. i., p. 120.)

To Saïd Ibn Djudi, a poet of the ninth century, we are indebted for a few couplets which in delicacy of sentiment could not be put below many of those of the troubadours or minnesingers of the twelfth and thirteenth :

" Since I have heard her voice, my soul has fled from me ; the enchanting sound has left me but regrets and sorrow."

" I think of her, and ever but of her, my dear Djehana; we never met, my eyes beheld her never, and yet I made her a surrender of this heart."

"Her dearly cherished name, which I prize above all, I'll now invoke with tear-dew in my eyes, as the monk calls on the image of his saint."

The pain of separation is thus celebrated in a few verses from the pen of Abul Fadhl Iyad :

"Since I beheld thee last, I've been a bird with broken pinions. Ah, could I but wing my way to thee beyond the sea ; for our separation will be the cause of death to me." (Dozy's Histoire, vol. ii., p. 228.)

Ibn Hazem, one of the celebrated names of the eleventh century, has left us not only a variety of couplets belonging to this rubric, but also a most charming account of an early love, evincing a delicacy and simplicity of feeling not unworthy of the time of Boccaccio or Goethe. This Arabic *novella*, for which we are sorry we have no room here, may be found in Dozy's Histoire, vol. iii., p. 344, *seq.*,* and in Von Schack, vol. i., p. 108–114.

Abu Aamir was an Andalusian poet, and Hind a lady of no less distinguished talent for poetry and music. Aamir had collected a little party about him (doubtless in some enchanting spot, for he speaks of the notes of nightingales around him), and there was nothing wanting to complete their satisfaction but the presence and the lute of Hind. Aamir therefore sent her

o The really classical love-story of the Arabs, however, and one to which the poets frequently allude as familiar to every one, is the extremely touching and idyllic history of Djemil and Botheina, which originated in the desert, probably during the first half century of the Caliphate. It is reported by Ibn Challikan, ed. de Slane, 169, and also by Von Schack, vol. i., p 37.

a polite poetical epistle inviting her to come, and to assure her of good company, promised her not only devout listening, but also the absence of every drink but water. Hind replied on the back of the letter, in the same measure and with the same number of verses, expressing her readiness to be present at so intellectual a *réunion.*

Almansur once sat in company with Vizier Abul Mogira in the garden of his magnificent country palais Zahira, and while both were taking their ease over their wine they all at once heard a fair voice commencing the couplets of a plaintive amorous ditty. Now it so happened that the voice was not unfamiliar to either of them ; for Almansur recognized it as that of the one he loved, while the vizier knew her to have a passion for himself. Abul Mogira therefore could not help referring the impassioned words of the fair singer to himself, and he was so imprudent as to reply to her in a few equally enamored couplets of his own. Almansur was infuriated, and thundered out the terrible inquiry : " Confess to me the truth, fair wretch ! was the vizier here the object of thy song ?" The lady did not hesitate to admit her predilection and appealed to his magnanimity for pardon ; she did so in a new series of verses, which she recited amid tears. Almansur now turned his anger towards the vizier, and loaded him with reproaches. The latter, however, although admitting his error, excused himself by saying that he could not help it, each one being the slave of his inevitable Fate, and his own in this instance happening to have been that he should love one he was not permitted. Almansur remained silent for a while, but finally magnanimously replied : " Very well ! then I must pardon both of you. Abul Mogira, the lady belongs to you ; I surrender her to you."

Hafsa, one of the fair poetesses of Granada, celebrated alike for her great beauty and her talent, had formed a sort of platonic *liaison* with the poet Djafer. But, unfortunately, the governor of Granada had also an eye upon her, and had become so jealous as to seek to destroy his rival. She was therefore obliged to use great caution, and when her friend once asked her for an interview she hesitated two months with her answer. Meanwhile Djafer, not knowing what to make of her long silence, wrote her a poetical epistle, still extant and full of tender melancholy and despair. The letter, which the author sent through his slave Assam, had no sooner reached, than the lady at once replied in the same metre and in the same rhyme, endeavoring to dispel his gloom and assuring him, that if he knew the ground of her reticence, he would cease to t. ccuse her. Hafsa gave her answer to the same slave that had brought the letter, but in dismissing him she artfully treated him so roughly, heaping reproaches upon him and his master both, that the poor messenger on his return bitterly complained of rudeness. The poet, however, on opening the epistle, found just the contrary, not only ample apology, but even the appointment of a rendezvous in his garden, and on that account pronounced his slave insensate. Presently the two really met in Djafer's garden, and when the latter was about to make reproaches, Hafsa hushed him by improvising : " Enough, that we are here together, and silent as in days gone by." (El Makkari, ed. Gayangos, vol. ii., p. 540.)

Abu Amr of Malaga, once happening upon a promenade about the precincts of his native city to meet Abdul Wahab, a great amateur of poetry, was asked by the latter to repeat for him some verses. He recited as follows :

" She has deprived Aurora of her blooming cheeks; she has received her slender form in feoff from Irak's fair-proportioned stems.
" She threw away her jewels to choose for her a better ornament, and put the stars about her neck, like strings of pearls, all bright and luminous."
" And not content with the light, graceful shape of the gazelle, she robbed the little animal of the sweet brightness of its eye besides."

Abdul Wahab had no sooner heard these verses than he burst out into an exclamation of admiration and fell to the ground like one in a swoon. On recovering, he said : " Pardon me, my friend ! There are two things, which always put me beside myself, so that I no longer remain master of my senses. They are, the aspect of a fair countenance and the voice of genuine poetry." (El Makkari, ed. Gayangos, vol. ii., p. 274, and Von Schack, vol. i., p. 240.)

In connection with this branch of Arabic poetry, we must not omit the names of Ibn Zeidun, one of the most eminent Andalusian poets, born about 1003, and of his Wallada, the fair and highly accomplished princess loved by him and celebrated in his verses. Ibn Zeidun's great talents had quite early in life elevated him to a very high position at the court of Ibn Djahwar, who after the downfall of the caliphate was for some time in power at Cordova. The poet enjoyed the most intimate confidence of his master for a great while and was honored with several missions to some of the smaller courts of Andalus. But he had also jealous rivals, and their machinations after a while succeeded in effecting his disgrace. The cause of this misfortune is supposed to have been his relations with Princess Wallada, who, as an enthusiast for poetry and

herself a clever writer of verses, had great respect for our poet
and openly preferred him to all the rest of her admirers. To
one of these her conduct gave so much offense, that he medi-
tated revenge and resorted to calumnies, for which after a while
he gained admittance to the ear of the commander. The con-
sequence was, that our late influential favorite was thrown into
a dungeon, and there remained confined, in vain attempting
through the mediation of a friend to recover the favor of his
angry patron. Yet he succeeded, after some efforts, in making
his escape from prison, and after having kept himself concealed
at Cordova for a while, he finally fled to the western part of
Andalusia. But the pain of separation from his Wallada and
the desire of living somewhere in her proximity did not suffer
him long to remain so far away, and he therefore soon returned
to Az-Zahra, one of the half-ruined palaces of the Ommaiades
near Cordova, where he entertained some hope of at least occasionally meeting with the madonna of his heart. He next led
a sort of erratic life, travelling at random through the different
provinces of Spain, until he at last settled permanently at Seville, where El Motadid received the weary wanderer with cor-
diality and honored him with princely confidence until the year
of his death, in 1071.

The Arabic anthologists are all of them extremely prodigal
of their hyperbolics in praise of Ibn Zeidun's charming ghasels,
which they maintain possessed of a power such as no magic
ever owned, and of a sublimity with which the stars could
never vie. And we must recollect that most of this poetry,
which was composed at different times and from different places,
had reference to his relations with Wallada, whom, as long as
he lived, he continued to celebrate with the profound devotion
of our modern Petrarch, and with the restlessness of Childe
Harold. We have thus another instance of a closer approxi-
mation to modern times than to the Christian poetry of the
Middle Age, and we have only to regret that our limits will not
allow us to produce in evidence some specimens (Von Schack
vol. i., p. 300–314).

One of the most prolific and attractive themes of the poets
of the West was the sacred wars of the Peninsula, in which the
Moors were perpetually engaged, and in which they evinced
scarcely any less ardor and self-sacrificing devotion than the
Christians. These wars lasted for more than seven centuries
with alternating success, which, however, at first, before and
during the caliphate, was generally on the side of the Moslems,

while after the fall of the Ommaiades the Christians gradually and steadily won more and more of the ascendant. But such was the pertinacity of Islam, that its existence on the soil of Spain was no sooner periled than new hordes of fanatical barbarians came streaming to its succor from Africa, and the contest became only so much the more fierce and destructive. There is thus scarcely a foot of ground on the Peninsula that was not moistened with the blood of the crusaders of both parties, and the number of those who fell in terrible battles like those of Zalaca, Alarcos, las Navas de Tolosa and others, amounted to hundreds of thousands, all of them firmly persuaded, on the one hand, of earning heaven with their devotion to the cross, and on the other of meriting Mohammed's Paradise as martyrs. The war, although originally one of conquest, yet after a while became a purely religious one on both sides, and on that account offers us a variety of curious points of contrast and resemblance. While the Christians scarcely ever prepared for a decisive engagement without on the eve of it celebrating the mysteries of the passion and partaking of the sacrament, the Mohammedans would on their part under the same circumstances spend entire nights in prayer and go on long pilgrimages to Mecca, to sue for the privilege of dying for their faith the death of martyrs. It was one of their traditions, that every one wounded in one of these battles would on the day of judgment appear with his wound bleeding; but this blood would be real blood only in color, and would exude a fragrance similar to musk. Nor was there any want of miracles on these occasions. On the eve of the battle of Alarcos, Abu Yussuf, after having spent the night on his knees, saw in his morning-dream a knight mounted on a snow-white charger descending from the sky with an immense green banner in his hand, who presently announced himself as an angel from the seventh heaven, coming from Allah to bring his faithful warriors victory. On the part of the Christians, it was Saint Iago, on whose patronage they mainly relied, and he was in more than one emergency more terrible than thunder and lightning to the Moors, who fled in terror and confusion whenever he was at hand.

Let us now see what the poets have to say about these wars, in which they themselves acted no inconsiderable part; and with what accents they at one time seek to enlist for the standard of the Prophet, and at another either celebrate a victory or give vent to lamentations over a defeat.

The following may serve as a specimen of the Arabic *prezicansa* or poetical exhortation to the sacred war, in which we will not fail to perceive at least as much earnestness and unction as in most of those of the Provençals. The author of it is Abu Omar, the secretary of Ibn ul Ahmar, king of Granada, at whose request it was composed and read to Sultan Abu Yussuf, to inspire the latter with new zeal for the war against the enemies of the faith. Its date is 1275, and we may add, that at that time the greater part of the Peninsula had already been subjected by the Christians.

"Here lies the path of safety. Is there one, be it in Spain, or be it in Africa, willing to enter it? who dreads Gehenna's flames, the torments of the damned, and longs for the eternal bliss of Paradise, where cooling shades and fountains are reserved for him? Thou, who art eager for victory in this our struggle for the faith, obey the impulse of thy heart! Go, armed with hope and confidence to meet salvation: and since thy cause is noble, there will be success. . . . Delay not; for who can assure thee of thy life to-morrow? The time of death is never known to us; but rest assured, thou never shalt escape the payment of the debt from which no mortals are exempt. If not to-day, thou yet must soon expect to leave thy place. The journey before thee is difficult, and one from which there can be no return. Be up then, and to ease the hardship of the road, supply thyself with an abundance of good works! And recollect, the first and most important of pious works is this our sacred war for the maintainance of our faith. Improve then the precious opportunity, and move at once to combat on the soil of Andalus. For God loves and rewards the one who dedicates himself to such a fight." . . .

"Who follows the example of the Prophet? . . . Who's ready now to flee to God, and by combating for him to purge his soul of the contamination of his sins? Can ye take pleasure in the cities of the enemy, which do not pray to Allah? Will ye endure it, to be derided by the believers in three gods, who hate us for firmly adhering to but one? What have we not already suffered from the rabble! How many mosques of our land have been converted into churches! O, the disgrace! Do ye not die from the chagrin, when ye are witnesses to it! The bell hangs now on our minaret; the priest is seen standing on its roof, and wine flows in the house of Allah, alas! nor is the voice of the believer any longer heard in it. . . . How many men of our nation, how many women, are languishing in chains among them, longing in vain for ransom from their dark dungeons! How many maidens, who in their distress can see no savior but their death, are mourning desolate in Christian cities! How many children, whose parents weep for having given life to little ones to be tormented! . . . How many martyrs, laid low by the sword, have not, as corpses of wounds without number, covered the battle-grounds! The angels of heaven will on beholding it drop tears of sorrow, nor can men whose heart is not of rock, be witnesses to all this misery without compassion. . . . Do ye not recollect our old alliance, our consanguinity! . . . And were the Christians ever too indolent to unsheath their swords, when vengeance called for it? Alas! the pride of Islam is extinct,—that pride, which once so nobly glowed. Why do ye hesitate thus in despair? Do ye expect a sword to wound, unless ye draw it?"

"You are our neighbors, ye Merinides; let therefore now your succor be the first! The war for our common faith is your first, highest and most sacred duty. Neglect it not! And choose one of the two, the glory of victory or martyrdom! Then will the Lord vouchsafe you rich reward, and fairest maidens will receive you in his heaven. The black-eyed *huris* of his Paradise above are even now ready to bid you welcome! Who then will offer himself now as Allah's combatant? Who'll purchase of him heaven's eternal boon? Allah has pledged protection to the faith, and never has his word been broken. . . . Ye are God's host, strong enough, if ye but will it, to subdue the world; and for the true religion can ye now but sigh and silently lament instead of acting? How could ye dare to appear before the Prophet. if he were to invite you now? Have ye excuses, were he to say to you: ' Why did ye not succor my people in distress, when it was so maltreated by the enemy?' Could ye escape the punishment, were ye with shame to hear this from his lips? Beseech him therefore to remain your mediator on the dread day of judgment. and fight now valiantly for his faith! Then he'll conduct you, brethren, safely to the pure limpid fountains of his Paradise." (Ibn Chaldun, vol. ii., p. 288; Von Schack, vol. i., p. 155.)

Another, and in many respects even a more eloquent and elevated kassida of the sort was composed by Ibn ul Abbar, who, when in 1238 Valencia was sorely distressed by the Christians, was commissioned by the alcayde of the city to go to Africa to the court of Abu Zekeria, one of the most powerful of its princes, to solicit his assistance. Our poet-ambassador had no sooner arrived than he recited his kassida in the presence of the entire court, on which, we are told, it produced so deep an impression that the prince at once conceded the desired succor by sending a well-armed fleet to operate upon the Spanish coast.

Nor is there any lack of kassidas commemorating the victories achieved by the Moslem arms of Spain and the glory of the chiefs that conducted them. When Abu Yussuf, for example, directly after the battle of Ecija, was entering Algesiras, he received from the prince of Malaga a poetical address congratulating him upon his victory. We have here room only for a few passages from it:

"The four winds have already brought us tidings of thy victories, and the stars, as they rise in the East, have been the messengers of thy success. The space was narrow for all the angelic host which brought thee help, O chief, and the wide battle-field did not contain them, while from the circling spheres above the song resounded: 'The Lord shall be thy succor in all thy plans.' The life, which each of us would gladly purchase with his own, thou hast thyself devoted to the service of the Highest, the Eternal One! Thou tookst the field for His religion, protecting it, relying on the prowess of thy unbending mind, as on a sword; gloriously was then thy undertaking crowned by thy successful army, and thou hast now achieved a work which never shall be dissipated into naught. . . . How majestic is thy army. O prince, when in the roaring din of battle the swarm of eager chargers surges onward, and the lances break and whistle all around! Thou art God's legate, leading his sacred cause, and his protecting eye is therefore ever upon thee; may it never fail watching! Thou hast adorned the faith with new, unfading splendor, and time will not be able to rob thee of the honor of such lofty deeds! . . . May He, whose faith thy sword defended, in his benignity now shield thee against every harm, and may he so abundantly upon thy head his blessings shower, that their fragrance may endure as long as time shall last." (Von Schack, vol. i., p. 153.)

3

The laments over the reverses of Islam are no less eloquent, and sometimes extremely delicate and pathetic. Such are, for example, those relating to the loss of cities, like Valencia, Seville, and others, for a specimen of which we refer the reader to Fauriel's History of Provençal Poetry (English translation), page 454, and to the "Journal Asiatique," vol. iv. of the First Series.

While the Spanish Moslems were thus celebrating their heroic exploits with all the studied rhetoric and gorgeous imagery of the Orientals, the rest of Europe was scarcely beyond the crudest beginnings of poetry, with the single exception of the Provençals, who at an early date commenced to rival their antagonists in spirited compositions relating to the sacred war. The Castillian was not sufficiently advanced for any such purpose, and its earliest crude tentatives, the ballads on the Cid do, not date farther back than the twelfth century, and could in point of art not be approached to the elaborate finish of the Arabs. In speaking here of the renowned champion of the Spanish *romanzas*, we cannot refrain from noticing in a few words the great contrast between the Arabic and Christian accounts of him. While among the latter Cid Ruy Diaz el Campeador (as his full name reads), is invariably represented as the model of every chivalric virtue, kind, affable, honorable, and always loyal even toward his unjust king, the Arabs give him the character of a perfidious and cruel barbarian, who fought neither for his king nor his faith, but in the service of some of he small Mohammedan princes. In this light he appears more especially in connection with the siege of Valencia, which he conducted, and where, after its surrender, he perpetrated the most atrocious barbarities, condemning the alcayde to the stake, and menacing his wife and daughters with the same. "This terrible calamity," says the account, "filled all classes of society with pain and shame. Nevertheless the power of the tyrant kept constantly increasing and rested heavily on hill and dale, inspiring all the inhabitants of the Peninsula with dread. . . . And yet this man, who was the scourge of his time, was, in respect to ambition, sagacity, and firmness of character, one of the miracles of God. He died shortly after at Valencia a natural death." (Dozy's Recherches, and Von Schack, vol. i. p. 161–171.)

We have already more than once alluded to the encomiastic poetry of the Arabs, which they were so often called upon to write in honor of their princes, and of which in the course of centuries there must have been an enormous number of pieces. We have now a word or two to add upon this point. It is a singular fact that in these compositions the poets of every period of their history adhere much more closely to the classical models of the Muallakat than in any other, and that on that account the reminiscences of the old poetry are made to occupy so conspicuous a place as sometimes to be entirely out of proportion with the object proposed. Descriptions of nomadic life, idyllic love-scenes, or amorous laments are therefore scarcely ever wanting, and it sometimes seems as if the poets of Andalusia's luxurious courts and enchanting landscapes were nevertheless longing for the old desert as for a better home. The princes themselves are not unfrequently addressed as if they were nomadic chiefs, and the poet likewise speaks of himself as of an Arab of the olden time. These preliminary amplifications often occupy so much of the kassida as to leave but a subordinate place for the encomium proper, which generally comes in at the end. In the panegyric portion, in which the poet seeks to celebrate the valor, the liberality and princely splendor of his patron, his naturally incurs the danger of becoming artificial, extravagant, or even bombastic; but although this is really the case with many, we are perhaps no less often surprised with an energy of expression and a boldness of imagery which we must recognise as classical. Let the following verses, addressed by Abdrebbihi to AbdurrahmanIII. prior to his assuming the title of caliph, serve as an example:

"The Lord in his benignity has opened widely now the way to Islam, and men are pressing, crowd upon crowd, on towards the road of mercy. On their behalf the Earth adorns herself for fairer habitation, and shines resplendent as if arrayed in silk. The cloud, O caliph-son, would cease to rain, were it to witness the kindly munificence, with which thou know'st to bless; and were the war to see thee leading thy hosts to battle, it would despair of stirring equal courage in others' breast. Before thee heresy falls prostrate and suppliant upon the ground; and since thou rulest, the horses willingly obey thy reins. The victory, O prince, is tied indissolubly to thy standards, when or by night or noonday they float before thee in the breeze of thy career; and thy refusal will rouse the caliphate to anger, if thou, the scion of the illustrious line, dost not thyself put on thy head the crown of the great Emir of the Faithful." (Von Schack, vol. i., p. 200.)

To this specimen we may be permitted to add another, addressed by Ibn Hani to some other prince. It is, however, much more hyperbolical:

"Before thy horses, when they storm onward to the assault, there are no hills, no mountains, however lofty they may tower up. They're known by being always foremost in the race, but no eye ever can pursue them, as they advance. The lightning knows of them. that they ride on its wings, and that in swiftness they excel even thought. The clouds, which towards the north pour down their fullest streams, are vanquished into shame before thy magnanimity's abundant showers. Thy right hand seems to touch and guide the very stars of heaven, as they emerge from lowering clouds of rain." (Ibn Challikan, ed. de Slane.)

One of the most distinguished poetical representatives of Granada was Ibn ul Chatib, from whose pen we have an entire divan of verses left us. He was prime minister and vizier to both Abul Hadjadj and his son Mahommed V., several times ambassador, and upon Mohammed's dethronement his companion and eloquent advocate at the court of Fez. To this court he had some time before been sent on a mission, to implore, in behalf of his master, Sultan Abu-Inan, for aid against the Christians, and this aid he obtained together with many compliments and presents by the recital of a poetical address, of which the following is the purport:

"Legate of Allah! may thy renown augment and exalt itself, as long as the moon's placid rays dispel night's darkness, and may the Supreme Ruler of our fate in his benignity ever defend thee, when dangers lower against which human power proves unavailing. Thy countenance dispels the midnight gloom, which sorrow casts around us, and thy hand showers refreshment on him who languishes distressed! Long since would our people have been expelled from Andalusia's lovely plains, hadst thou not with thy host dispensed abundant succor. But one thing now is needful for our Spain, potent commander,—but this one,—that thou shouldst send without delay thy army to our strand. to save us and to avert the threatening cloud." (Ibn Chaldun, Histoire des Berbères, vol. ii., and Von Schack, vol. i., p. 335.)

The satire was scarcely any less zealously cultivated by the Arabs of Spain than the panegyric, and their kassîdas of this category are often so elaborately constructed as to be a running parody on the eulogistic. Their satire, however, is rarely objective, that is to say, levelling at the vices or foibles of men in general, but almost invariably personal and determined by special situations or events. The weapon was, therefore, a generally dreaded one, and yet it is remarkable to observe, how often and with what degree of license the poets made use of it, not only against each other or their equals, but even against the mightiest of those in power. We thus find Hisham's impotent administration sorely castigated, in spite of the terror of its dreaded regent Almansur, and El Motadid of Seville is ruthlessly caricatured by Ibn Ammar in a long kassîda in the shape of a regular parody on the encomiastic. In a shorter piece, directed against a member of his own craft, Ibn Ocht Ganim advises him "not to be so impudent as to sip of the drink of which he is not worthy, and not to soil the noble art of poetry with kisses from his lips." From this we must not imagine, however, that the poet was always safe in the employment of so perilous a weapon. Ibn Ammar was subsequently cruelly assassinated, although for another much graver offense, by El Motadid's son, while Abul Makshi, as we shall presently see, lost both his eyes on account of some offensive allusions to a prince of the time of Abdurrahman I.

That the charming sky and the enchanting landscapes of Andalusia did not fail to produce their effect on the imagination of the Moorish poets is manifest from a great diversity of pieces descriptive partly of scenes and other objects of nature, partly of some of its numberless works of human art. Andalusia itself is sung in terms of the most glowing eulogy, and lauded as the terrestrial representative of Paradise. We meet with verses on the rivers, the Guadalquivir and the Guadix, on the rock of Gibraltar, on moonlit evenings amid fairy gardens or ruined palaces, on the orange-groves of Seville, on flowers, stars, landscapes and fountains, in short, on every thing which the poet's fancy could invest with interest or life. Boating-excursions on the rivers, especially of a calm clear night, are frequently dwelt upon with manifest delight. There is scarcely a variety of flowers, on which there are not some ingenious verses, especially on the violet, which to the Andalusian was the harbinger of an eternal spring. If the object described happened to be a work of art, such as a palace, the verses, if they were especially approved, were inscribed in letters of gold upon the walls of the monument thus celebrated, as we may at this day yet see them in some of the villas of Sicily or in the halls of the Alhambra.

In spite of the prohibitions of their religion, the Moslems of Spain seem nevertheless to have been any thing but abstinent of wine, and, if we may credit the poets, to have passed the cup freely at every hour of the day, sometimes even early in the morning. But their drinking seems to have been rarely solitary or intemperate; it was rather convivial and linked to social merriment, to poetry and music. This is evident from their many drinking-songs, some of which are extremely spirited and lively, and not unfrequently a jovial defiance of the law. Thus El Motadid proposes a new commandment, enjoining on all true believers to drink early in the morning, instead of listening to the muezzin, and Ibn Hazmun somewhat waggishly derides the anchorites and dervishes on account of their hypocrisy in this respect.

> "The use of wine is in itself no crime: the crime is but the terror of the law, or else even our dervishes would dare to moist en their dry palates with the cup."
> "When during the night they've muttered prayers until their throats are hoarse and sore: say, do they not themselves then reel like wanton camels o'er the sand?"
> "My house is therefore like their cells; yet maidens, slender as gazelles, are my muezzins, and I use cups to light it, instead of lamps."
> (Von Schack, vol. i., p. 218.)

That the Moorish poets, however, gay, light and fanciful as they naturally were, could yet also be of a much graver tone of mind is evidenced by a multitude of elegies and pieces of a religious turn, of which not a few must be ranked among their most finished and successful compositions. From some of them we have poetical prayers, which often evince no little earnestness and depth of feeling combined with great beauty of execution; from others religious couplets of a different sort, as for example, verses which the poet would write before his death with the request of having them inscribed upon his tomb; and of these pieces some are considerably longer and more elaborate than the mere epigram. Reflections upon the instability of human life, repentance over past offenses, and hope in a divine mercy most generally constitute the simple circle of ideas within which they moved. That many of these compositions must have been highly prized and even used as prayers is evident from As-Suhaili's assertion in reference to one composed by himself, of which he says every one that had made use of it to ask God for some favor had met with the fulfilment of his wishes. We have room here for a few of the concluding verses:

> "I have no other refuge but that of knocking at thy door; and if thou openest not, then I stand powerless and hopeless in my woe. O Lord, whose name I praise now and invoke in prayer, if thou dost not vouch-safe to grant thy servant what he sues for now, do not on that account plunge the poor sinner into complete despair; for boundless is thy benignity and infinite thy mercy." (Ibn Challikan, art. As-Suhaili.)

In the department of the elegy we might produce a host of specimens, had we space for them; but we must be contented with a few. A very beautiful one of upward of fifty verses adorns, in the shape of an epitaph, the tombstone of Abdul Hadjadj Yussuf, one of the kings of Granada, who fell by the hand of an assassin while in the act of prayer at the mosque.

It is quite symmetrical in its composition and commemorates in many a pathetic distich the nobility, the virtues, the valor and achievements of the deceased, and his untimely fate. A few verses of it may suffice :

" In the flower of his manhood and at the zenith of his power he was made to fall, like Omar, by the decrees of Heaven. There is no blade, no lance, on which we can depend as a protection against the will of Allah, and every one who builds upon the fleeting vanities of earth, will, undeceived, at last perceive that he has built on sand. Therefore, O Ruler of the kingdom which has no end ; Thou, who commandest every one of us and predeterminest his lot, vouchsafe to spread the veil of thy benignity over all our faults ! For, without thy compassion we all would have to tremble before our guilt. And lead the Emir of the Faithful, enveloped by the robe of thy boundless mercy, into the mansions of eternal bliss. True happiness and life that never ends can only be found with thee, O Allah ! The world is but an evanescent show, which, as it deceives, destroys itself." (Von Schack, vol. i. p. 213.)

An elegy on his own blindness was composed by the unfortunate Abul Makshi, who lived at the time of Abdurrahman I., and was most cruelly deprived of his eyes at the command of Prince Suleiman for having in some verses addressed to him allowed himself some offensive allusions to his brother Hisham. On having finished his piece, the poet obtained admission to the caliph and recited his verses, by which, we are told, Abdurrahman was moved to tears, and gave him two thousand dinars, one thousand for each eye,—a compensation, to which Hisham himself after his accession was so compassionate as to add an equal amount (Journal Asiatique, 1856, No. II., p. 476). Among the Moors themselves, the elegy composed by Ibn Abdun on the fall of the dynasty of Badajoz was one of the most highly prized, but it is too elaborate and artificial to be equally to our taste. Among those which are really pathetic and sublime we may again mention that on the decline of Islam in Spain already spoken of on page 34. It is from the pen of Abul Beka Salih, and was occasioned by the taking of Cordova and Seville by Ferdinand the Catholic.

Among all the compositions of this class, however, there is perhaps nothing more beautiful and touching than the elegies written during his imprisonment by El Motamid, the unfortunate emir of Seville, and we can therefore scarcely refrain from reproducing a specimen or two from them. But we have in the first place to premise a word concerning the most romantic life and adventures of this prince.

El Motamid was a member of the glorious dynasty of the Abbadides, which for a long time elevated Seville into rivalry with the Cordova of the caliphate, and which in every respect was one of the most brilliant centres of Moslem civilization in the West. He was the son of El Motadid, who commenced to rule in 1043,—a cruel and most treacherous sybarite, but nevertheless a great amateur of poetry and himself a writer of verses. In early youth El Motamid was fonder of his enjoyments than of his arms, and a culpable defeat before Malaga, where he had been sent to fight, incensed the father so much, that the young prince had no little difficulty in escaping from his punishment to Silves, where he then lived for some years in exile, until he finally appeased the wrath of the offended parent by addressing to him a number of poetical epistles. He had, however, on sooner succeeded to the throne, in 1069, than he not only at once evinced a much nobler temper and a far greater poetical talent than his father, but he also presently proved himself much more of a warrior by the conquest of Cordova, which he then added to his kingdom.

The first period of El Motamid's reign was one of the sunniest prosperity, and he was so brilliantly surrounded by every thing in the shape of material and intellectual refinement, that the historians of the West have almost as many anecdotes to relate of it as those of the East have left us concerning the life of Harun ar Rashid.

" El Motamid," says Ibn Challikan, " was the most generous, hospitable, magnanimous and powerful of all the princes of Spain, and his court the most popular place of repose for travellers and the resort of talent of every kind; in a word, the point upon which the hopes of all were centred, so that no court of any other ruler of that time could boast of being frequented by an equal number of poets and men of learning." And in all this El Motamid was far from being a mere Mæcenas or an idle spectator; his intellect was as alive and active as any. It was during these halcyon days of his existence that he improvised a series of poetical effusions, which in point of natural ease and graceful elegance are not inferior to any of his time, and of which his biographers have left us a minute account. All of these pieces originated at some one of his favorite places of resort, palaces in the city or on the river, such as El Mubarak, El Mukarram, Az-Zoraya, Az-Zahi and several others.

The first shadow cast upon this Eldorado life of El Motamid was the tragical death of his son Abbad, whom he had appointed governor of Cordova, but only, it would seem, to lose him in an insurrection led by Ibn Okasha, a native of the city.

The father was frantic and ordered the rebel to be nailed to the cross (a punishment which some time before he had attempted to inflict on a thief), suspecting but little how many additional calamities he had yet before him, to which the present was but the ominous prelude. About that time the cause of the Christians had been making new advances, and Alphonso VI. of Castile had succeeded in making all the Mohammedan princes tributary to his power, El Motamid included. But not content with the payment of tribute, Alphonso after a while sent an embassy to Seville demanding of its king a surrender of his fortresses. This was too much for our El Motamid, who in his indignation beat the ambassador and ordered his companions executed. The outrage naturally gave rise to new preparations for war, and the siege of Seville was contemplated. In this emergency the Moslem sheikhs, afraid of combating Alphonso's force alone, concluded to apply for aid to Yussuf Ibn Tashfin, the king of Morocco, and in 1086 El Motamid himself went over, to be surer of success. Yussuf agreed, and at once collected a large force of cavalry and foot, with which he shortly after won for his confederates a most brilliant victory in the bloody battle of Zalaka (1086), from which Alphonso had a narrow escape. But Yussuf was as treacherous as he was cruel and fanatical (he had sent the heads of tens of thousands of slain Christians to the different cities of Spain and Africa), and returned to Africa only to plot treason against his allies on the other side. After a series of preliminary manœuvres, in which he yet pretended to be El Motamid's friend, he finally threw off the mask completely, and after the capture of fort Tarifa commanded himself proclaimed master of Andalusia in 1090. He next took Cordova, in the defense of which Mamun, one of El Motamid's sons, lost his life, and then Seville, which its king defended only with the loss of an additional son, and where he presently had to witness all his palaces devastated by the fanatically barbarous enemy. El Motamid himself was taken prisoner with his entire family and sent in chains to Africa, where he was doomed to spend the remainder of his days in a dungeon at Agmat, a city some distance southeast of Morocco. In this condition he remained until he was released by death in 1095. One of his daughters was subsequently sold into slavery at Seville and one of his grandsons became a jeweller somewhere else in Spain.

The keen reverses of fortune experienced by El Motamid did not fail to produce a profound impression on his mind, and he almost sunk beneath the weight of his afflictions. Yet he endeavored to console himself, like a man of intellect and heart, by giving vent to his grief in a series of poetical effusions which we have already characterized as elegies, and which are yet esteemed as among the most perfect of his nation's literature. They generally link themselves either to some reminiscence of his former life or to some incident of his imprisonment, of which his biographers offer us a minute account. A flock of wild pigeons, for example, passing by the window of his dungeon, gave rise to the following reflections :

"As in my sorrow I witnessed the pigeons flying by my prison, I thought, while tears descended from my cheeks : ah, they are not in chains, are not incarcerated, like myself! And, by the eternal heavens! I thought not so from envy,—no, only from the desire of being free and happy like themselves, able to move about wherever I might wish ; that heaven might grant me the boon of happier fortune like their own, and I not here in solitude might be obliged to languish in my chains, heart-broken and deserted. Alas! these pigeons, who know no sorrow and whom no distance separates from their kind,—they do not, like myself, pass dreary nights in terror, nor is their mind disturbed with apprehensions, like my own, when the gaolers approach my door and move the clattering bolt. Thus Fate has from eternity decreed it over me, that I should end in prison, deprived of all the dignity and splendor of my reign! Let whoever may, love life, loaded by the weight of chains! As for myself, I can do nothing in my distress but long most ardently for my deliverer in death. But as for you, dear pigeons, may God protect you, and may no falcon rob you of your young, as they've robbed me, whose anguish ever bleeds anew, when I reflect how ruthlessly my dear ones have been torn from me."

On hearing one day, that one of his sons had headed a revolt in Andalusia against the robber on his father's throne, he improvised the following :

"And must my sword-blade thus grow old without a blow, although I daily brandish it, eager for combat ? And must my lance thus rust in indolent repose, instead of tasting red blood from the enemy, and thirst in vain after its wonted drink ? And shall the charger of the unhappy prince never again foam underneath its rider ? No! it never will again obey my reins to hurry me onward ; for it has shuddering scent of enemies lurking concealed in ambush. But, if none have pity on the sword, to satisfy its languid cravings for its drink; if it be fated that my polished lance-point shall grow diseased from shame, unable to endure its disgrace,—then mayst thou, Mother Earth, at any rate soon have compassion on thy poor sorrow-stricken son ! Vouchsafe thy child a little place upon thy bosom, and let him in the grave find ample repose !"

In one of these elegies, El Motamid contrasts the clinking of his chains with the music of the fair singers by which he once was surrounded. In another he laments over the loss of a cherished son, and over the wretched aspect of his daughters, whom he perceives disfigured by hunger and in rags, obliged to earn their livelihood by spinning at Agmat—one even at the house of some one formerly in her father's service. But on these couplets we have no room here to dwell. We will content ourselves with a few more passages from his lines to Az-Zahi, the superb and beautifully located palace on the Guadalquivir, where he had spent many a delightful hour :

"O'er me, the prisoner on Maghrib's strand, the orphaned throne of my dear country weeps; so do the pulpits of the mosques in Spain weep over my calamity. The sword and lance, which once I brandished high, are now draped in deep mourning o'er their loss, and Fortune, which on others smiles, has fled from me. . . . O, were I, free from chains, once more permitted to see my home and its familiar retreats! O, could I pass again, as formerly, my nights along the rapid Guadalquivir, reposing in the olive-thicket near the pond, while round me the soft evening-breezes dallied with the branches of the myrtle and in its foliage the turtle-dove cooed her sweet song! And that my eyes again might light upon Az-Zahi's and Zoraya's majestic piles! Could they but see me, they would delighted stretch out their pinnacles, like arms, to meet me, and my Az-Zahi would in eager haste long to embrace me, as a groom his bride! But all this now seems quite impossible to me, and yet God sometimes works even the impossible."

Among El Motamid's cotemporaries we can scarcely omit mentioning the equally talented and excentric adventurer Ibn Ammar, whom his genius raised from the obscurest origin to the command of armies, the intimacy of princes, nay, to the eminence of princely rank itself. He was a poet of no ordinary merit, although of a skeptical turn of mind ; in succession the confidential vizier, the ambassador, and chief commander at the court of Seville, and for some time the royal governor of Silves, but by his ambition misled into treason, and on that account eventually murdered in prison by the hand of El Motamid himself.

In addition to the varieties of poetry thus far enumerated, the different anthologies offer us several others of the minor sort, such as epigrams, gnomic verses, apophthegms and inscriptions of every shade and hue, besides an immense number of pieces that do not admit of definite classification. From these we might select many a specimen of ingenuity or elegance, perhaps even many a literary curiosity, were our limits not already passed. To the drama and the epos the Moslems of the East and West and of every period of their history remained almost entire strangers, and even of the epic ballad or romanza, as it existed in Christian Spain, and much earlier in northern Europe, there is scarcely a real vestige to be found among them. And the reason of this was not because there was no popular poetry among them, but because the origin, the development and genius of their poetry was a peculiar one and in fact entirely *sui generis.* As to the existence of a popular poetry, that is to say, of a poetry of and for the masses and in the common dialect, and that of a very extensive one, among the Arabs of Spain, there cannot be the slightest doubt; for not only, as we have already seen, was even the peasant behind the plough ambitious to make verses, but there are also several distinct poetical varieties or forms, such as the *zadjal* and the *muwashaha*, which are designated as peculiar to the people, and in which the poets of the court not unfrequently wrote pieces destined for a wider circulation among the millions at large.

Among the Moslem poets of Andalusia it is customary also to include those of the north of Africa and of the islands, especially of Sicily, where there was a large number, and some of them of considerable distinction. Such was, for example, Ibn Hamdis of Syracuse, from the eleventh century, one of El Motamid's friends, and the author of a great variety of pieces of far more than ordinary merit, among others of several long kassîdas inscribed by way of ornament upon the walls and ceilings of one of Prince Almansur's superb palaces at Bugia. Blind and unfortunate in his old age, he compared himself to the eagle no longer able to fly, and to whom his young are obliged to fetch his nourishment. To the name of Ibn Hamdis we may add, as likewise of Sicily, those of Ibn Tubi, Ibn Tazi, Bellanobi, Abul Arab, Ibn Kaffa, Ibn Omar, Ibn Daw, and Abdurrahman of Trapani. The entire number of Western poets, of whom Von Hammer-Purgstall has given biographical notices with specimens of their writings in the fifth, sixth and seventh volumes of his history, amounts to upward of three hundred and thirty.

One of the most prominent and striking peculiarities of the poetry of the Arabs both of the East and West is, as we have already observed, its originality. It developed itself from the outset entirely out of its own resources, and never at any period of its history did it become subject to any foreign influences whatsoever. To such an extent is this so, that one of their most learned and cleverest writers, Ibn Chaldun, probably only repeats hearsay, when in his chapter on Arabic poetry he alludes to that of the Persians and the Greeks and speaks of Aristotle as mentioning and praising Homer. It is true, that the Arabs have enjoyed the reputation of having known the Greeks at a time when elsewhere in Europe they were entirely forgotten, but their knowledge was confined almost exclusively to philosophical and strictly scientific works, and these even they derived not from the original, but from some Syriac translations at their command. In every other respect, that is to say, in every thing

relating to the history, mythology and poetry of other nations
they exhibited the most astonishing ignorance. What wonder
then, that a philosopher of no less eminence than Averroës
should in his paraphrase of Aristotle's Poetics substitute the
names of Antar, Amrulkais, Montenebbi, &c., in place of those
of Homer, Euripides and Sophocles, and that he should have so
little conception of the character of Greek literature as to de-
fine tragedy "the art to praise," and comedy "the art to
blame," and upon the basis of this monstrous assumption to
claim for the panegyric and satirical kassîdas of his nation a
place by the side of the high tragedies and comedies of the
old Greeks?! Nevertheless, however true it may be, that the
Arabs on account of their adherence to their own antecedents
and their neglect to learn from others, should have entirely failed
in the highest forms of poetry, it is yet equally undeniable that
in those forms which they cultivated and developed among themselves. which we have seen to be the lyrical, they really rose to
a very high degree of perfection, and that they have left us
gems and flowers without number, which will lose nothing in
comparison with any other of their kind, either ancient or
modern.

The question concerning the influence of the Arabs on the
poetical literature of the South has occupied the historians and
critics for a great while, some claiming nearly every thing,
even the rhyme, derived from them, while others are disposed
to credit them with nothing whatsoever. The truth lies doubtless somewhere between the two extremes. For while on the
one hand we can not evade admitting the existence of a long
protracted, if not an intimate, contact between the two civiliza-
tions upon the soil of Spain and Sicily, however hostile they
otherwise were, especially in respect to religion, and a contact
that extended itself to every class of society, it is on the other
hand no less manifest that the Christian poetry of the Provençals,
of Spain and Italy has every characteristic of a distinct individuality, and of one which can only be accounted for by assuming
it to be an original and inherent one. Let us adduce a few
facts of the case :

Although the Christian authors of Spain of every century
are but too prone to pronounce judgment in reference to the
Moors indicative of the grossest ignorance, denouncing even
their scientific men as necromancers in league with the devil,
and contributing in every way to fan the religious hate which
formed one of the most deeply rooted characteristics of both
parties, it is yet equally evident that a large number of Chris-

tians of every rank and in every part of Spain found in the natural course of events better opportunity to judge of their antagonists, and that in many instances they had occasion to be rather favorably than otherwise impressed by them. In many cases (and these in the course of centuries must have been quite frequent), in which sections of Christian population were conquered or led captive, and mildly treated, the natural result was free, if not friendly, intercourse, and this often lasted so long that many of them learned not only to speak, but even to read and write the Arabic, and to compose verses in it, while on the other hand the unfortunate Moriscos must to some extent have likewise found opportunity to make known their language and perhaps now and then also their poetry among their conquerors. Sometimes the conquered Christians were free to the extent of complete religious toleration. At different times many of them served in the army of the caliphs or kings, while others occupied lucrative places at court or in the palaces of Moslem nobles. Under these circumstances it is not surprising that the refined culture of the Arabs should occasionally attract them likewise to its circle, and that after a while the more educated among them should despise their unwieldy dialect, the rustic Latin or Romansh, and apply themselves with avidity to the language of their masters. Such was the case as early as the ninth century, if we may credit Alvaro, the bishop of Cordova, who complains bitterly of it as a great calamity to the church. "Many of my religious cotemporaries read the poetry and the tales of the Arabs, and study the writings of the Mohammedan theologians and philosophers, not to refute them, but in order to learn how to express themselves with correctness and elegance in the language. . . . All the young men, who are noted for some talent, know but the language and literature of the Arabs; they read and study Arabic books with avidity; nay they even go to enormous expense in collecting libraries of them and every where declare the literature to be a most admirable one. . . . Many have even forgotten their own language, and there is scarcely one in a thousand amongst us, who knows how to write a tolerable Latin letter to a friend, while scores of them can express themselves most elegantly in the Arabic, and even compose poems in this language better than the Arabs themselves." Of poems of this description there are yet some vestiges extant, and we also know that in Andalusia the Latin was at one time so far neglected that Archbishop John of Seville found it necessary to translate the Bible into the Arabic. Nevertheless we must not imagine that this was the

case every where ; the *rustica* or Romansh continued to exist
quite generally as the idiom of the people, with which in their
turn then the Arabs were likewise sometimes familiar. It is
needless to multiply examples ; it is not necessary to remind
ourselves of characters like the redoubted champion, the Cid,
who fought alternately under kings of both parties, although
always claimed faithful to one, and who was doubtless familiar
not only with the language but with every thing relating to the
civilization of his ally-opponents ; we have evidence enough to
prove that Christian Spain was not beyond the reach of some
influence from so conspicuous and popular an element of
Moslem culture as was their poetry. In Sicily the contact,
although later, is yet equally apparent, at least as long as Frederic II. and his son Manfred kept imperial court upon the island.
Frederic was from early youth familiar with the Arabic, the
friend and munificent patron of high scientific culture in general,
surrounded by men of science and letters from all parts and of
every sort, of which, we are expressly told, quite a number, if not
the majority, were Arabs, and some troubadours from the South
of France. Now Frederic was not only himself an amateur of
poetry, but he enjoys the fame of having introduced the Provençals upon Sicilian soil and of having thus founded there a school
which at a little later date merged itself into the Italian ; and how
could a prince of Frederic's taste and society remain a stranger to
the poetry and the poets of a nation, in which in other respects
he found so much to appreciate, and on a spot where the superb-
est architectural monuments were considered ornamented
by inscriptions from the hand of genius ? But besides all this,
we have evidence of even a direct influence of the Arabic
element upon the old Spanish or Castilian in a number of popular pieces which have been shown to be refusions of Arabic
zadjals and *muwashahas* yet extant. Any farther than this,
however, the influence of the Arabs has not, and in all proba-
bility can not, be proven, and we must therefore assume it to
have been much more of an indirect and general than of a special
or radical one. The poetry of the South of France, of Spain
and Italy is therefore nevertheless far from being a borrowed or
ingrafted one ; it originated and matured on an essentially different ground, is the expression of a distinct circle of ideas, and
in point of both form and substance bears the imprint of a pro-
foundly marked individuality.